THE TAVERN OF LOST SOULS

Alan Britt

Červená Barva Press
Somerville, Massachusetts

Červená Barva Press
P.O. Box 440357
W. Somerville, MA 02144-3222

www.cervenabarvapress.com
Bookstore: www.thelostbookshelf.com

Cover art: Vincent Van Gogh, The Night Café

Cover Design: William J. Kelle
Author Photo: Charles P. Hayes
Production: Steve Asmussen

ISBN: 978-1-950063-26-0

Library of Congress Control Number: 2022942668

CONTENTS

2

3

4

THE TAVERN OF LOST SOULS

Appreciation to those who offered encouragement throughout the writing of this book: Steve Barfield, Alberto Blanco, Brooke Bognanni, Zoltán Böszörményi, Mary Beth Britt, Heath Brougher, Nilda Cepero, Flavia Cosma, Niza Fabre, Red Focks, Paula Gottschalk, Clarinda Harriss, Charles P. Hayes, Claude Morency, Roberta Crawford Morency, Dzvinia Orlowsky, Scott Thomas Outlar, José Rodeiro, Paul B. Roth, Silvia Scheibli, Steve Sleboda, Paul Sohar, and Kahlia Williams

Special gratitude to Gloria Mindock for her patience and unerring support for this project

About the cover: Vincent Van Gogh characterized his painting, Le café de nuit (The Night Café,) as "A café where night prowlers can take refuge there when they have no money to pay for a lodging, or are too drunk to be taken in."
[Yale University Art Gallery]

Acknowledgments

The poems (sometimes in earlier versions) in this book appeared in the following publications. Grateful acknowledgement is made to the editors of those publications:

Ann Arbor Review: "To a Catbird"

The Bitter Oleander: "The Dark Horse"

Blue Fifth: "Ode to Tuesday"

Bolts of Silk (Scotland): "December, 2002"

ByLine: "In This Day and Age"

The Coe Review: "Alien Religion"

Crucible: "Ode to the Fifth Amendment"

The Cultural Journal: "White Spruce" and "Sunday Night"

Danse Macabre: "Autumn Wasps," "Beethoven," "The Heretic," and "Waiting for Cicadas"

decomP: "Ode to a Rainbow"

Eskimo Pie: "White Spruce," "Sunlight," "If I Only Had a Brain," "The News as It Is Today, June 13, 2003," and "Communal Love"

Eunoia Review: "Restless Night," "Another Dream," and "Truth in Symbolism"

Fullosia Press: "Christmas Poem, 2002," "December, 2002," "Evolutionary Christmas," "New Year's Eve," and "Happy Holidaze!"

Gloom Cupboard (United Kingdom): "Crickets"

Home Planet News: "Ghost Story"

Praxilla: "Sipping Yellow Tail Shiraz in Early June"

Queen's Quarterly (Canada): "Bringing Pablo Home from a Second-hand Bookshop" and "Dreams"

Radiant Turnstile: "Miguel Hernández," "A Poem that Should Have Been Called the Foot Against the Drum," "Poem that Begins with a Pink Neon Hand Blinking in a Fortune Teller's Window," "Jules LaForgue," and "True History"

The Recusant (United Kingdom): "Tango Dancers," "Today's Recipe," "Alien Existence," "Reading Baudelaire on Sunday," and "The Cicadas of 2004"

Refined Savage Poetry Review: "Noon" and "The Tavern of Lost Souls"

Sawbuck: "Incognito"

Scythe: "Mexican Singer" and "Ode to a Cobra"

The Sound of Poetry Review (Greece): "Remembering Spot, Amber, Shasta, Chanelle, and Jacques," "A Poem for the 17-Year Cicadas and My Brother," "48 Days," "The Persona," and "Last Dance"

Straightjackets: "Bulletin," "Sunday Night," "Ode to James Wright," and "The Crooked Afternoon"

Strangeroad: "Gnats" and "For the Lost Poets of New Orleans Who Frequent Mardi Gras"

Unlikely 2.0: "With Time to Kill in the Midst of a Crisis" and "Thinking About Illusions"

* * *

"Thinking About Illusions" appeared in *Unlikely Stories of the Third Kind: Best of Unlikely 2.0* edited by Jonathan Penton, Make It New Media LLC, Unlikely Books: El Paso, TX: 2010.

"Autumn Wasps" Translated into Romanian by Flavia Cosma for *Vatra Veche* (Section Biblioteca Babel): 2013

* * *

"August Dreams" and "Autumn Wasps" in *Alianza: 5 U.S. Poets in Ecuador* (bilingual anthology in English with Spanish translations by

Ricardo Pérez-Salamero García, Alex Lima, Lilvia Soto, and María Teresa Azuara), Alan Britt, Editor, CypressBooks, Rio Rico, AZ: 2015

"Ode to a Rainbow" and "The Tavern of Lost Souls" in *Resurrection of a Sunflower,* Catfish McDaris and Marc Pietrzykowski, Curators, Pski's Porch Publishing, Lockport, NY: 2017

"The Tavern of Lost Souls" in *The Music of the Aztecs: Poets of the DC Magic Theater Poetry Club,* David B. Churchill, Editor, Pony One Dog Press, Washington, DC: 2019

* * *

"With Time to Kill in the Midst of a Crisis," "Ode to James Wright," "Autumn Wasps," "Dreams," and "Communal Love" in *Parabola Dreams* (Poems by Silvia Scheibli and Alan Britt), The Bitter Oleander Press, Fayetteville, NY: 2013.

"Communal Love" in *Violin Smoke / Hegedűfüst* (English/Hungarian: Translated into Hungarian by Paul Sohar), Zoltán Böszörményi, Publisher, Iradalmi Jelen Könyvek books, Budapest, Hungary, 2015

Poetry about Anything and Everything: *The Tavern of Lost Souls*

Equally rebellious and passionate, Alan Britt is, in my opinion, the quintessential American poet. His universe easily encompasses far away galaxies and alien existence as well as people at hand, domestic life, animals, gardens and skies, myriads of cicadas, enchanting birds, and humble insects. His poetic sensibility vibrates at the intricate beauty of nature:

> I believe these white flowers
> belong to the camellia or wild rose
> families, somehow,
> flapping their crocheted wings
> at the sight of April
> sauntering in the nude
> past our open dining room window

Britt's poetry is situated at the border between his awe in front of the sensuousness of natural wonders surrounding us: "Outside, heavy humidity rubs her breasts /against all eight window panes," and the fascination with the vast universe and its occupants:

> They're able to store all information about their culture
> from antiquity to the present on something the size
> and shape of a marble.
>
> . . . each marble composed of complex
> information threads swirling the middle
> of a mauve cat's eye database.

In his poetic visions gardens are exploding with the abundant spring of life, an ALIEN universe is bursting into ALIEN existence and/or vice-versa, the poet's burning questions about the origins of our lives poignantly haunting his readers:

. . . think about ancient ancestors, strangers, lovers,
all who've ushered you
through the swinging doors of alien existence.

Now, how do you feel about gardens,
seeing as how this one's barely three weeks old?

Never a stranger to the pitfalls of human condition, the political strife or the plight of the humble, Britt would always take a stand in favor of the weak, the oppressed, the misunderstood, and the misfit:

Finally, just around midnight,
a shabby guitarist, with crescent
moon scar on his forehead
and a busted hip, saunters
into the tavern of lost souls.

Alan Britt masterfully plays with time, space and the mighty universe as a lonely kid would play with his oversized, slightly ragged toy. Under his attentive watch time compresses when it comes to miracles and dreams that abound in youthful images of an expectant love only to disappear again and again, forcing the poet to a bitter return:

to my original room
on the other side
of my flimsy dream,
only to see myself
staring back at me
in that same sliding glass door's
rippling mirror

Stubbornly, the author looks for a solution to preserve his cherished illusions:

> we should devise a convenient place
> to store our dreams,
> so that we might recall them,
> reactivate them as necessary
> on our most dismal of nights,
> on our saddest of nights,

Chased by ghosts, followed by unfulfilled desires, the poet philosophizes about illusions:

> Well, truth is that illusions every day
> get crushed beneath the supple hooves
> of a mountain goat's flowing white hair
> that resembles an angel recently escaped
> from the local Catholic church.

Nostalgia, abandoned souls, suffering and joy, shattered dreams that somehow refuse to die, dead poets and holy saints, all find their rightful place in Britt's compassionate and healing words that "are begging for roots / beneath a razor-thin solitude."

Always an optimist, the poet recovers his eternal smile and immediately declares

> Ah, but the emotional energy between words,
> a reality that glitters
> behind the cleansed doors of perception

(those five mischievous sisters)
while fueling the appetite for younger poets pushing violins
through their curly walnut hair.

These poems are another splendid accomplishment by a prolific poet who verily states that "to write poetry is to love and to love is to write poetry."

—**Flavia Cosma** is a Romanian-born Canadian poet, author and translator. She is the Director of the International Writers' and Artists' Residence at Val-David, Quebec, Canada and the Director of the Biannual International Festivals at Val-David.

I

This thirst that has me by the throat,
How much would it take to kill?
As much as it would take to fill
Her tomb – that is to say, a lot;

~Charles Baudelaire

(Trans. by William H. Crosby)

Gnats

Now I'm going to tempt my bones
with this Chablis.

For now, keep on circling
that orange tin jack-o-lantern;
yet, I've a feeling my French companion
won't go unnoticed by your micro-orbit.

But what bizarre lust possesses you
to backstroke my chilly goblet of solitude
this third week of April?

A celebration?
Birthday of sorts?
Time measured by sensations?

Or perhaps it's your passionate nature,
in general,
your immanentist lifestyle?

I believe you possess
a Rimbaudian sensibility,
one that plunges you headlong
into this French wine, diving
below her waist of stopped clocks,
and making you far more human
than I cared to realize.

With Time to Kill in the Midst of a Crisis

For 20 years I've never discerned
these twisted white flowers
in late afternoon twilight that filters
our gauze dining room curtains.

Outside, heavy humidity rubs her breasts
against all eight window panes.

I believe these white flowers
belong to the camellia or wild rose
families, somehow,
flapping their crocheted wings
at the sight of April
sauntering in the nude
past our open dining room window.

Sipping Yellow Tail Shiraz in Early June

Well, I know you,
33% moon.

I've seen you before,
eyeball
peeking through the magnolia's billowing
pale pink kimono.

You linger a mythical
Greek forest
between laurels
spanning 12,000 generations.

Still, why have so many
overlooked you
in favor of the quarter moon,
(whom I've coveted myself),
or the half moon
in her low-cut, black pearl nightgown,
or the debilitating bare shoulders
of the full moon?

33%, you are alive,
rustling as a fish
between the magnolias.

And for that I offer you a toast
of Yellow Tail Shiraz!

Alien Religion

So, that takes them back to the year 150,000 BC,
if you're using Jesus as a Fahrenheit thermometer.

They're able to store all information about their culture
from antiquity to the present on something the size
and shape of a marble.

And to think they have the most sensual flecked silver
on hand-blown cobalt goblets filled with marbles
representing every discipline ever encountered
in their culture . . . each marble composed of complex
information threads swirling the middle
of a cat's eye database.

Of course, these aliens never used a Fahrenheit thermometer,
and they've never heard of Jesus.

Alien Existence

The garden's leafy jade muscles,
its designer absinthe perfume,
its wild flowers' purple teeth grinding the outer edge
of a wire fence,
its addiction to youth,
its cayenne peppers filled with gunpowder,
and its lusty eggplants parading magenta make-up
in morning-glory torn jeans.

This garden is about to explode!

Chili peppers and yellow tomatoes alone could spell doom
for thousands ordering exotic drinks in Purgatory.

So, take a moment and think about all the monarchies
that beheaded or burned intelligence at the stake,
sociopaths that drew and quartered the bloody seams of consciousness,
then think about ancient ancestors, strangers, lovers,
all who've ushered you
through the swinging doors of alien existence.

Now, how do you feel about gardens,
seeing as how this one's barely three weeks old?

Another Dream

In my dream
I watched you
through a sliding-glass door,
smiling, waving
to let me know
you're still alive.

I went looking for you.

Yes, I left my room,
circled the drizzling patio
to your room,
and slid open that glass door
only to find your room empty,
vacated abruptly
revealing your shabby apartment's
ghostly walls,
celery curtains,
and straw-colored carpet
slightly stained
by youthful
expectations.

My shoulders felt the weight
of anemic shadows,
since I knew
I'd been had.

So, I returned
to my original room
on the other side

of my flimsy dream,
only to see myself
staring back at me
in that same sliding glass door's
rippling mirror.

Ghost Story

How come ghosts
leave no scent?

I often hear them
rummaging my neighbor's garbage,
disturbing the raccoons.

One ghost
smells like sea grapes
nudged by July's arthritic fronds
sifting the ochre sands of Palm Beach
while mint waves
shatter their white teeth
against pink sea walls.

But you said ghosts leave no scent?

That's true.
I did say that.

Another ghost tastes like perfumed ribbons
of indigo smoke swirling a long clay opium pipe
cradled between Thomas De Quincy's wilted fingers.

There you go again!
No scent, you promised!

That's true.
I did say that. I remember now.

Ode to a Rainbow

I haven't seen a rainbow like this one forever.

Seven Van Gogh palette knives smearing
parrotfish scales across the horizon.

Know any good poems about rainbows?

Me either.

Ode to a Cobra

Two saffron drops smear death's walnut hood that
resembles a housewife beneath a commercial hair dryer.

The housewife's reptile eyes say we must face destiny,
even though destiny is often a banal misperception.

Until that fateful day we caress destiny's purple hips
swaying like giant eggplants in the June garden.

Ode to James Wright

We read James Wright's poem in class today,
the one about him lying in a hammock,
listening to cowbells, detailing dragonflies,
wasting his life.

Student response was robust.

In the south corner of our room
John Keats engaged in conversation
with Wordsworth; I wanted to eavesdrop
but was interrupted by Shakespeare,
Aleixandre and Neruda chatting
beneath a thatched veranda
in Lake Worth, Florida.

Later, as James rolled from his hammock,
students followed him
to a fence along that pasture
where his Indian pony awaited them
with the patience of Saint Judas.

Bulletin

Well, I guess Trent Lott's *Hooray for the Grey!* speech
didn't go over so well.

Republicans are about to lose some business.

The White House is already shining the shoes
of the next Senate Majority Leader.

Mississippi wonders if they should even reclaim Trent
after all his bad publicity.

While Democrats are busy sharpening their claws
on the leafless cherries that line Pennsylvania Avenue.

Christmas Poem, 2002

Blade of sunlight through Shiraz
ignites flamenco hips.

Spider clicks scatological claws
inside a cardboard box scudding
a musty basement corner.

Responsibilities are often taped
inside cardboard boxes, then dragged
onto a bluewhite lamplit curb.

Ah, but today, December sunlight
migrates the patio and fondles
the waist of my devoted Shiraz,
embracing her melancholy hips.

December, 2002

Whoever heard of a photograph
staring back at you,
making you uncomfortable?

I mean, what's that all about?

Making you nervous
like you needed to perform
some bureaucratic duty?

Damn photograph just found me
deep in December.

Evolutionary Christmas

Doves emerge from corn husks
to sip pear nectar
from our Christmas tablecloth
strewn with pumpkins tumbling
through a dark green universe.

Tiger-striped gourds and oak leaves
litter this vinyl field of imagination
as tendrils form a fist
of grapes
that struggle
like souls careening
below their watery depths
among mollusks and sea slugs
to redefine evolution every
ten billion years or so.

New Year's Eve

(*Into the dangerous world I leapt,*
Helpless, naked, piping loud;)
~William Blake

Then Dom Perignon enters
to shake hands with white fingertips
before laying white gloves across left forearm
to deliver another howling,
bloody new year.

Happy Holidaze!

Murdered by crows from the imitation
German wall clock's twisted walnut shell
and beveled glass window reflecting splinters
from a crystal chandelier onto your champagne
curls as your lips drip scarlet tanagers when
you divert your attention just to be coy.

2

Hope is the light that through the windows of the Inn
Gutters before it dies forever.

-Charles Baudelaire

(Trans. by William H. Crosby)

To a Catbird

Fat raindrops pour from the gutters of your thoughts
like propane changing from gas to liquid or the way
a tiger moth completes metamorphosis by pumping
wet shadows into her orange-spotted wings.

A gunshot or backfire muffled by a rainforest
of dripping maples on this chilly Sunday twilight—
a motorcycle's purplegreen abdomen, like dawn's
sheen on houseflies, nibbles the nearby intersection.

Fat raindrops pour from the gutters of your thoughts
as an empty freight train plows its rhinoceros horn
beneath Platonic aberrations that have been
sustaining coal for many generations now.

Bringing Pablo Home from a Secondhand Bookshop

Sometimes words, Pablo said
when he was just about my age,
help to focus our lives.

They create universes,
governments,
new religions,
clock repair shops,
and bakeries thick with the aroma
of fresh imagination.

Somehow these words
look backwards,
forwards
and to both sides
illuminating lives, deconstructing epiphanies,
while launching satellites into our mysterious universe.

Speaking of words, earlier today when that yellow bird
emerged from a single grain of pollen
in one of your poems, Pablo,
I felt your words *vibrate* all the same!

Thinking About Illusions

(*I chose my own illusion…*)
–Pablo Neruda

Since illusions are doled out like bouquets
of canary, iris and mauve flowers
stacked in white plastic five-gallon buckets
waiting at the next intersection.

Well, truth is that illusions every day
get crushed beneath the supple hooves
of a mountain goat's flowing white hair
that resembles an angel recently escaped
from the local Catholic church.

Green chirrups riot the canopy
of our fabulous maple who's been
quite the tyrant these past few days
with her glistening wet leaves
creating perpetual dusk.

A male cardinal injects morphine
into the late afternoon's jade shoulder,
followed by six drops of mercury carving rivers
below the Christian icon's paint-peeled eyes.

Noon

Green lips.

Baroque chimes announce 12 PM.

Accordion weaves rust and golden threads
of cannabis through a folk tapestry.

Appaloosa enters this dream—
its cinnamon splotches shiver
cold reality.

In This Day and Age

The military trained politician swirls his finger
around the rubble of archaic thoughts,
triumphs new settlements along the West Bank.

It's impossible to know just how long
this is all going to take,
but we know we're almost home!

Still, the irrational resistance of natives
is both annoying and fatiguing,
It's like splitting the atom!,
he offers with a crooked smile.

So, pock marks along the walls of irony prevail,
while young women, faces buried beneath illusion,
waists strapped with dynamite,
prepare to blow up maple trees along a backyard
somewhere near Reisterstown, Maryland,
torching orioles like sparklers on the verge of reproduction
as TV antennas wave their anemic wrists of despair
and pump black dreams, wet and helpless, from cocoons.

The only hope left for this planet
hinges on a few poems by Pablo Neruda,
about a mermaid, sock weaver, clock repairer,
plus anyone relegated to an HMO waiting room.

Restless Night

I'm not the same person I was,
rest assured.

And I'm no longer the person I wanted to be
for so many years.

That, too, is evident.

But exactly who I am today isn't clear, either.

So much happens overnight.

Ode To Tuesday

She misses my descent completely,
mowing with her back to the western sun.

Chewing rectangles of grass, oval by oval.

White breeze disturbs the magnolias
this warm summer evening,
dragging behind it the smell
of finches and fresh laundry.

If I Only Had a Brain

If we use only 10% of our brain, as experts say,
then we have all those extra brain cells
waiting to be mined like amethysts.

There's so much brain going to waste
they ought to give some of it away
on the Price Is Right
or Wheel of Fortune.

Just think what we could do
with all that brain!

We could enjoy world harmony for starters,
not that harmony's a priority these days,
but, remember, we're only using
10% of our brain right now!

Eventually we could transcend space and time.
But, hmm . . . would that diminish Andrew Marvell's
wonderful "Definition of Love"?

I've got faith in the remaining 90%!

Yes, I believe we could crack the acorns
of religious rhetoric's fossilized psyches,
since words are terrestrial symbols chosen
to medicate panic existence in the first place.

Words shape consciousness, though,
and most things associated, like truth,
lies, unnecessary grief, auto accidents,
and whatever transgresses our daily lives.

Words are minted in unlimited-limited editions
then marketed over cable TV.

Words are sold from university podiums,
then pawned and mass-produced in the form of banal stories
for our children.

Words are legalized,
pasteurized,
lumped together
and horsewhipped
begging for roots
beneath a razor-thin solitude.

Ah, but the emotional energy between words,
a reality that glitters
behind the cleansed doors of perception
(those five mischievous sisters)
while fueling the appetite for younger poets pushing violins
through their curly walnut hair.

With total brain power
our heads would be so far gone;
our heads would be mind-melding with other galaxies
and reading their poets,

absorbing their music
which somehow has found a way
to combine all five senses
into a singular physical sensation,
one that ignites all the senses
simultaneously,
thereby establishing a
unique experiential reality
tasting of metal and amaranth.

So, the expanding brain's the way to go?

Now, I suppose our biggest concern would be
how to make the expanding brain more *profitable*,
more *advantageous*,
in order to manipulate the seasons,
control lightning,
and nudge killer hurricanes toward enemy shores.

The News as it is Today, June 13, 2003

"Ode to My Socks" is as profound
as "Prufrock."

Different nuances, of course.

Creativity takes a myriad of forms.
Against all odds, human imagination
surprises, even overwhelms.
Sometimes it's hard to imagine the obstacles
that a humble man or woman overcomes
just to maintain simple existence.

Like gypsies, people emerge from the fog
with entire lives on their backs,
families huddled,
the elderly collapsed against
whatever allows them peace.

I believe one day, when thunder becomes symbolic again,
then and only then we'll discover
the true nature of existence,
heralded by trumpets, snare drums and guitars lit like green fuses,
plus lusty violins with the wings of palmetto bugs,
and Seminole artists pressing mystical tiles into the walls
of North Palm Beach seafood restaurants,
or from a high school, Baltimore County,
a ghostly-pallored student
writing poems that dream of breaking
the sound barrier—
all these and more could erupt

into one glorious moment right beside
adults aiming their remotes at the national news
(those environmentally controlled regions of consciousness)
with the sound of an 87-billion-dollar gavel doling
out judgement as we've come to know it today.

Crickets

Crickets, carnivorous stars
below a lonely moon.

Crickets' thick choruses billowing
this way and that with trills resembling
blueyellow beaks rattling a Peruvian rainforest.

The half-moon kneels below green maples
to spread her mother-of-pearl nightgown
over white lawn chairs and bare shoulders
of a split-rail fence.

While crickets, industrious and hopelessly
immune to personifications in their midst,
continue chewing tiny holes in the ragged
nightgown worn by this humid July moon.

Autumn Wasps

Wasps surround your floppy straw
bonnet this early afternoon.

Each striped thorax
resembles dying sunlight.

As you shake your walnut hair,
wasps bob like tassels the bonnet's edge.

A middle-aged poet in Habana
dreams beneath a 36" fluorescent tube.

You shake your walnut hair again.

Wrinkled legs follow you inside the apartment
of that poet scribbling poems in Habana.

You share a bottle of Australian Shiraz
and talk about the old days.

Beethoven

For all his ferocity Beethoven
wrote the sweetest melodies.

He balanced his entire generation
on a single piano key.

Stole from the past
to create the future.

Ate like a madman,
chewing, composing,

and observing flirtations with
the subtlety of a chicken hawk

guarding the gilded hallways
of the Count's opulent palace.

White Spruce

Snow crows
squawk and squawk
atop a snowy spruce.

Automobiles bruise
the dirty white hips
of February.

The Dark Horse

I must've been dreaming
if I thought that whale oil scallop shell sconces
flickering my imagination's stucco walls
were real.

I was rudely
elbowed
in the ribs
when your guitar
rode past
on its cloudy Leipzig stallion.

I was half-crazy
to believe
I could escape
the passing
Mardi Gras
undertow.

But there is one thing.

I've learned that if you fondle the flowing walnut hair
of verbs paled by whale oil long enough,
you'll discover
imagination
to be a welcome source
of illumination
while tunneling the hideous intestines
of enlightenment.

The Tavern of Lost Souls

About the color of amber
asleep in a drawer
at a North Dakota fossil lab
an ant descends the crack
of a sidewalk
just below
my approaching Reebok.

I carry the shadow
of Nagasaki
in my walk.

However, my true agenda
is not cruelty.

As a matter of fact,
each morning around 12 PM
the mayor of my village
walks his burro
past the Chamber of Commerce.

Women make important decisions
while our men drive SUVs
to the local reservoir
in search of the Wild Man.

(Fewer capital crimes
are committed this way.)

Adolescents, mute since birth,
stitch fantasy tattoos
across each other's shoulders and lower backs
with the lethal precision of André Breton
and Tristan Tzara.

Extended families mingle
the local watering hole.

They cross their shriveled legs
while lighting up a stick
and growl into muddy drinks
all various shades of amber
asleep in drawers
at a fossil lab
somewhere near North Dakota.

Until, finally, just around midnight,
a shabby guitarist, with crescent
moon scar on his forehead
and a busted hip, saunters
into the tavern of lost souls.

The Crooked Afternoon

(. . . *the crooked afternoon* . . .)
~James Earl Jones

It all begins innocently: clock guts
hanging inside-out.

Jacques, our Bouvier the color of cognac,
scratches twice the aluminum patio door—
wants in from the rain.

As he enters the kitchen, large drops
of quicksilver from his wooly fur shatter
our chilly mocha Andalusian tiles.

3

My readers will find no difficulty in translating these forms of the outward senses into their intellectual analogies.

~Samuel Taylor Coleridge

The Heretic

(*You must look inside yourself in order to realize salvation.*)
~Jesus of Nazareth, according to the Gospel of Thomas

The Heretic enters a Temple, overturns tables
littered with coins imprinted with Caesar
and assaults dogma cowering behind holy robes.

The Heretic speaks a rare truth.

Suddenly we're back in AD 33
believing we can live without the sword;
but Romans didn't give up that easily,
and neither will we.

The Heretic speaks a rare truth
and for this he will be vilified,
unfairly scrutinized by the media,
and crucified at least ten thousand more times.

Dreams

(For Chanelle Vida Britt)

(*...the river*
which as it grows deeper
is seen to run slower, clearer.)
~Miguel Hernández

Ever notice how dreams
each passing hour, day,
month, year disintegrate
as though eaten voraciously
by piranha or algae?

I suppose that makes perfect sense;
otherwise, we'd be overcome by dreams.

Where would we store
all those dreams?

In shoeboxes
stacked like designer bricks
across the top shelves
of our closets?

We're overrun by boxes!

But these dreams
could be useful,
what with the price of cable TV
constantly rising.

We need a back-up plan!

I'm telling you,
we should devise a convenient place
to store our dreams,
so that we might recall them,
reactivate them as necessary
on our most dismal of nights,
on our saddest of nights,

on a night with shallow breathing
through the leafless maples,
on a night with melancholy shoulders
like tonight.

Miguel Hernández

(*It takes work and love.*)
-Miguel Hernández

Miguel Hernández, boney damselfly,
elbows pointing to the sky
above a florescent cobalt torso,
relaxes upon my ax handle today.

Miguel Hernández, boney damselfly,
with bulging indigo eyes
scouring the deadly horizon,
relaxes upon my ax handle today.

A Poem that Should Have Been Called the Foot Against the Drum

In the quasi-commotion
of the under-populated
international foods aisle
with its absurd jarred vegetables
and seductive fruits,
just before the Spanish guitar
flicks its tongue
across a young girl's ribs,
(young girl adjusting
to an unbroken string
of broken hearts),
and just before the boomslang harmonica
disguised as a violin
comes coiling, coiling,
coiling.

Communal Love

(For Ruxandra Cesereanu)

First, the French doors click,
then my bones,
and suddenly lights flicker
like a spirit tangled
in low ceiling fixtures
while passing through this basement room.

The guitar is purely Mexican.

The guitarist's fingers,
tarantulas
tugging the pouting lips
of the senora cantata.

Piano keys,
ice falling
from a wedding veil.

This ice quickly scooped
from the glistening counter
by a swift palm,
by elaborate machine guns.

In any event, the mistress
enters the subterranean bar
with a swagger
and melting stars on her shoulders.

Death looks her straight in her eyes
and she doesn't even flinch.

Tango Dancers

Revolutionary
by nature—
their scorpion waists
in love
with the black moon.

Poem that Begins with a Pink Neon Hand Blinking In a Fortune Teller's Window

(*No one has seen us. We have seen*
no one, blind as we are from seeing.)
-Miguel Hernández

The hand flashing neon pink
against a shop window,
five fingers spread,
with its infinite melancholy roads,
is a map of freedom, some say.

Others say it's a hoax.

This hand held before your face—
is it waving goodbye
or hello?

Does it speak in tongues
(in this case vibrating pink fingers)
or does it merely smear broken relationships
across the creases below your eyes?

So, looking into a mirror
you would see more clearly
the illusion of your life?

Your heart like a scrap of metal
lies on its side, refusing to beat.

But the hand beats,
it pulsates darkness,
wanders the sidewalks looking for innocents
while avoiding
the retired professor, the one who once carried Merwin and Donne
in his briefcase secured by two baby alligators.

The blinking hand has no use for the professor
with one foot in welfare
the other boxed and padlocked
in rental storage shed
while the city inspector prepares paperwork
for the real estate financier
who, strangely enough, began as an earnest student
of poetry with the now defunct professor.

Well, the hand with pink neon fingers
vibrates a shop window
also about to be foreclosed
by the real estate financier.

Where does all that energy come from,
fleecing the timid and the poor?

Why is the shallow life more enticing
than reading Merwin and Donne?

Even innocent school girls about to be deceived
by the pink neon hand about to be foreclosed
prefer a shallow life
over the raspy insights of Merwin and Donne.

Electricity from the pink neon hand
arcs when gripped
by the hand of the real estate financier
and carefully pried finger by finger
from the shop window.

On the sidewalk the hand lies shattered.

Each finger pulsates
in haphazard direction.

It has become a Cubist hand.

So, that is how art is born, by accident,
by cruelty, by greed, by crushing each
of the pulsating pink neon fingers
until only one finger remains
blinking, blinking, blinking.

Ode to the Fifth Amendment

I love Pablo Neruda;
therefore, anything people say
could be held against me.

No sooner do I plead the Fifth
than my grandfather rounds the dusky corner
of blue gravel Carlyle Road in Tampa,
Florida, past blazing palmettos
and pregnant grapefruit trees
to announce his dented green
Dodge pick-up has just received a new clutch.

Uncork the doorstop—
fresh blackberry wine for everyone!

Jules Laforgue

People wore
Jules Laforgue t-shirts
long before Mick Jagger
growled into a microphone.

I first remember riding with Jules
in his white '67 Corvair;
that's when I discovered him
cruising South Dixie Highway
at speeds I'm no longer proud of.

Surviving a decade of disco
and greedy capitalists,
Jules lost a little weight—
hair whitened
he now wears inexpensive drawstrings
to assure maximum comfort.

Recently, I spotted him, again,
Veteran's Stadium, Philadelphia, 2000,
wailing *Not Fade Away,*
raging against the universe,
as usual.

If I could afford it now,
I'd too wear boxers and t-shirts,
swim trunks,
even three-piece suits
emblazoned with the logo of Jules' raw,
insolent and sarcastic barbed tongue!

True History

(*History is important. If you don't know history, it's as if you were born yesterday. And if you were born yesterday, anybody in a position of power can tell you anything, and you have no way of checking up on it.*)
~Howard Zinn

You know, it's easy to escape true history.
When they eventually find a way to regulate every synapse of pleasure,
or monitor love now living as the Loch Ness Monster
dripping its head above the mythical lake of existence,
we're going to find ourselves
drowning in lead-lined nets tossed by our dead ancestors,
before realizing that we're near to
but otherwise struggling toward far more desperate shores.

Truth in Symbolism

(For David and Judy Ray)

Imagine the symbolism
on their horses
and Native American attire
going into battle at Little Big Horn.

They had lives, cultures,
infant daughters to protect.

Each horse adorned
with red, white and yellow paint.

Each stroke of paint
a symbol of anger, frustration,
ultimate revenge.

Ochre palm-prints
across the flanks of his pony
Crazy Horse was already
yelling at the government
the way Allen Ginsberg would
almost 100 years later.

Liberation! That's it!
The liberation promised
all along.

And, then, the innocent cavalry,
comprising the usual assortment

of naïve young men,
rode in
on government horses
branded and alphabetized
in a dog-eared, leather ledger.

It was no contest.
The symbols won.

As a matter of fact,
symbols win almost every time.

Until a posse corrals the symbols
snug as bedbugs inside their flannel
incognito pajama pants
watching Animal Planet,
the History Channel,
or NOVA special on Dian Fossey
communing with gorillas.

You see, symbols are an endangered species.

Some even believe they have their side
of the fence and should learn
to stay in their yard,
as Robert Frost suggested
almost 100 years ago.

But there's still time, I say, to pay attention
to the most symbolic thinkers
of our generation—
our poets.

Incognito

Over the very long haul
remember that all serendipitous
events fall apart.

It's inevitable.

As Blake said,
or Baudelaire,
or Lorca,
(who knows—
you could just as easily mistake an orchid
for a switchblade).

You could even,
with proper cultivation,
bomb-sniffing dogs, notwithstanding,
survive comfortably well into
the next millennium
fully incognito.

Remembering Spot, Amber, Shasta, Chanelle, and Jacques

(For Mary Beth and Chelsea)

You know when someone you love dies,
people say it feels like losing a part
of yourself?

Haunted by a grief swallowing asbestos
ceiling and sheetrock walls,
you're willing to bargain with the devil!

Well, when my dogs died, I would gladly
have given anything, a hand, an arm,
a leg, to save each one.

So, by now, I'd be armless, legless,
I know, and perhaps liverless, lungless,
and missing three kidneys.

Yes, that's how it feels.

4

What would we not give for some great poem to read now, which would be in harmony with the scenery,—for if men read aright, methinks they would never read anything but poems. No history nor philosophy can supply their place. The wisest definition of poetry the poet will instantly prove false by setting aside its requisitions.

~Henry David Thoreau

Reading Baudelaire on Sunday

When Baudelaire began a poem,
he didn't know where,
he didn't know when
it would end.

Sifting his way through human frailty
while paying attention to things lesser poets buried
beneath the borrowed sentiments of their age,
Baudelaire possessed infatuation
for language and misery.

And he wasn't one to avoid confrontation,
as his endearing consternation among
the intellectual effete testifies.

But Charles, Chuck, or Baudi, if you prefer,
had an uncanny arrogance
that scared the living shit
out of some people.

So, how serendipitous that he vagabonds
my dusty bookshelf this very afternoon,
in his white satin coffin, sipping absinthe,
prepared to spring upright,
indignant at the first sign of praise
for his paranoid genius.

A Poem for the 17-Year Cicadas and My Brother

So far we have one cicada
clutching the bottom of a weathered maroon 4 by 4
that supports our extended carport roof.

Upon closer inspection
I determine this cicada inclined
to split open its carapace,
its diminutive baked-potato husk.

I often see these husks, Pompeian fossils
imprinting the wrinkled bark, the elephant bark
of oak and maple trees.

I happen across them during solitary walks
through nature surviving my suburban neighborhood.

But any moment now
we'll be inundated
by cicadas exploding orange clay
across our Norway Maple's anaconda roots oozing
early May's lush green definition of love.

We're supposed to be annoyed
by the impending deluge of cicadas,
by this band of gypsies approaching,
as gypsies always want to relieve you of something.

There hasn't been this much trepidation
since Genghis and his buddies
devoured entire cultures

during the original wild west
that occurred in the east.

But I have a feeling
that these *belle canto* cicadas
are primed to deliver a bloodcurdling concerto
normally reserved
for Brazilian Leap-Year poets,
or my brother
prepared to dip his melancholy plume
below the vanishing ripples of his mercurial soul.

Waiting for Cicadas

A cicada wobbles sideways along arthritic wire
tacked to a faded oak fence.
His eyes fresh rust
or amber,
but not exactly the blazing red promised
by local news anchors.

He negotiates
each curl of wire.

His wings,
two stained-glass Baroque windows,
his torso,
perfect segments of palmetto bug imperfection.

Nearby, cicadas like compass needles in the eye
of a hurricane, cling to lattice.

Closer inspection reveals their eyes
as various shades of red,
from tulip red to a bruised ochre found only on salamanders,
from cayenne pepper red
to an apple rotting on the tree of despair,
and some even display the red promised
by local news anchors.

Ten feet away
another cicada wobbles a horizontal strand
of wire,
exposing her crushed wing.

Her wing of misfortune
wasn't meant for flying,
or was it, now?

We'll have to see about that.

Hell, it's barely 5PM.

Still, that nagging myth . . . that existential briefcase
filled with alarm clocks discarded
in our temporal universe urging us to awaken
from our 17-billion-year naps
and learn how to empathize.

Sunlight

Afternoon sunlight's
calf legs flickering
through cracks
of warped lattice
pause briefly
to chew the cuds
of dirty clouds.

Today's Recipe

(For Larry Ziman)

When you start with a pinch of melancholy,
then sprinkle powdered seaweed
mixed with organic carrots and California black kale,
well, surely, you understand the implications?
The result is the resurrection
of a splinter faith from the Cartesian well
of absolute truth,
that's a given.
But small price to pay,
I say,
for your shadow draped across a black walnut bar
smoking organic cigarettes
and ordering drinks
called "The Tyger,"
"the thorns of life,"
or "Blood Wedding."

For the Lost Poets of New Orleans Who Frequent Mardi Gras

(And for all those Primordialists out there)

You know we're forever writing poems
about our modern age enhanced
by printing presses, typewriters,
computers, and space age scanners,
but what about the poets
or near-poets
who for thousands of years
lived without an outlet
for their complex despair?

You know they existed.

These poets or near-poets
who survived blood-thirsty monarchies
by waving illusions the size of fists
through clouds of locusts
in a 4th century field of mud and millet.

These poets or near-poets
could tell us the truth
starting from prehistory
to Alexander, the Crusades,
and the genocide
of imagination
that's existed for millennia.

Trial by Ordeal—
how unimaginative can you get?

These poets saw it all,
the rape of the Magi and the indolence
of kings leaving the Magi's tent door
open for magpies to swoop down
from their scientific perches
and devour the Magi's succulent entrails,
followed by the systematic suppression
of women who lived as slaves to the slaves
of sanctioned hedonism.

These poets or near-poets
deserve a moment
of silence
for their lives without expression,
for their violent melancholy,
as we raise our red petroleum cups
above the outrageous human stream
flowing tonight down Canal Street,
brazen human stream
rattling the bourgeois suburbs
of New Orleans.

The Cicadas of 2004

You can smell their rotting bodies.

A humid smell of kitchen garbage about to offend,
inspiring its removal to the 50-gallon plastic can
with lid that fits like a fighter pilot's helmet.

While the odor isn't overwhelming,
I do check myself.

The pulsing decibels and layers of cicadas at this moment
resemble the metallic hues of a rainbow clinging
to the ragged pea-soup entrails of an abusive tornado.

There's this tremendous rattling of beads,
ten billion rattlesnakes stirring hibernation.

The whole thing resembles a universal pulse,
though no such pulse has ever existed.

Two mockingbirds manage their serrated discontents,
occasional oriole loops his whistle through a brief lull,
but not much else penetrates
this thick living wall,
this ecstatic chanting that first inspired Aztec myths.

And that omnipresent din deep in the background,
the sound of flying saucers from 1950s science fiction films,
aliens appearing docile at first
then advancing
the way rumors of the Mongol hordes
terrorized the sophisticated clergies of 12th century Europe.

But, today, these cicadas, through their mythological gills filter
the most wonderful atoms the universe has ever produced,
the atoms of Jesus, Blake, Gandhi, Neruda.

48 Days

The cicadas have returned!

(I need to get out more.)

After a meltdown and half-hour hiatus,
these cicadas return to full force.

Rattling, chanting their entire existence
reduced to these few weeks.

They've waited 17 years in the ground for this!
Don't think for a second
they won't chant for all they're worth!

Back in full swing
husks cling to everything:
picnic table, lattice, the carport's concrete floor.

Some sway in messy webs
strung from carport Havisham chandeliers
filled with damselflies, moth wings,
and fragments of oak leaves.

These husks are fecund, as Neruda might say,
covering our mythological universe
and leaving behind hollow traces
to indicate they barely existed at all,
while their true bodies, blazing, overshadowing everything else
on this earth for 48 days after a solid 17-year nap,
explode into ecstatic poems!

Mexican Singer

(For Chavela Vargas)

Her voice
of scorpion
and camellia
trembles the black maples.

With fists of pepper,
fists from the bloody crucifix,
fists emerging from her womb,
she strolls among us
incognito.

Sunday Night

(*Better run through the jungle!*)
~John Fogerty

Last night a speckled cobra coiled an olive
branch above my Scandinavian bed.

Tonight the Australian madman in khaki
shorts grieves over his lost crocodile, Mary.

Madman weeping for a soul as precious
as any sanctified bride could ever be.

The Persona

What're you doing there?

I'm looking for the poem's persona.

But, what if the poem has no persona?

What?

I said, what if the poem you're exploring
has no identifiable persona?

Well, I suppose those are still-birth poems,
or SIDS,
how sad that thought.

Still, that doesn't explain why you're here.

I had nowhere else to go.

No demand for tedious confessions?
No cocktail manuscripts close to deadline?

I don't believe I'm the victim
of anything you seem to value
with such indolence.

By the way, where'd you get that gorgeous
indolence of yours tattooing shadows
below the equator of your left breast?

Now you feel the persona's pouting lips,
her nutmeg curls,
her onyx eyes like caves
filled with two fists of wild pepper.

Her hips knock dust
from your malaise,
that melancholy matron
of your petulant youth.

Mark my words, you'll lust the persona's jade sparrows
when she exhales.

You know that,
right?

Thanks. I'll try to remember.

As I was saying (before rudely interrupted) moonlight
like a clouded leopard prowled your neck during
our night of rugged romance
in that after-hours supermarket parking lot . . .

Last Dance

In death we waltz as though returning
to our high school proms.

Carnations' cinnamon wings vaporize
into teeth marks, into a reflection
of blue alcoholic drinks trailing long
silk scarves across our faces.

And, yes, it appears that our silver '57
stuck headfirst in Farmer John's cornfield
was merely a serendipitous sign, after all,
of better things to come!

Notes

1) Section 1: Charles Baudelaire's quote from *Flowers of Evil and Paris Spleen* translated by William H. Crosby. Rochester, NY: Boa Editions, 1991

2) Page 16: William Blake's quote from his poem, "Infant Sorrow," in *Songs of Experience*, 1789

3) Section 2: Charles Baudelaire's quote from *Flowers of Evil and Paris Spleen* translated by William H. Crosby. Rochester, NY: Boa Editions, 1991

4) Page 23: Pablo Neruda's quote from his poem "El constructor/ The Builder." *Neruda: Selected Poems* translated by Anthony Kerrigan. New York: Houghton Mifflin, 1990

5) Page 40: James Earl Jones' quote from *Field of Dreams*, Universal Pictures, released April 21, 1989

6) Section 3: Samuel Taylor Coleridge's quote from *The Complete Works of Samuel Taylor Coleridge*, New York: Harper & Brothers, 1854

7) Page 44: Miguel Hernández's quote from his poem "El mundo es como aparece/The World Is as It Appears." *I Have Lots of Heart: Selected Poems* translated by Don Share. Newcastle upon Tyne, UK: Bloodaxe Books, 1997

8) Page 46: Miguel Hernández's quote from his poem "El mundo es como aparece/The World Is as It Appears." *I Have Lots of Heart: Selected Poems* translated by Don Share. Newcastle upon Tyne, UK: Bloodaxe Books, 1997

9) Page 50: Miguel Hernández's quote from his poem "El mundo es como aparece/The World Is as It Appears." *I Have Lots of Heart: Selected Poems* translated by Don Share. Newcastle upon Tyne, UK: Bloodaxe Books,1997

11) Page 55: Howard Zinn's quote from his book *A People's History of the United States*, Harper Perennial Modern Classics; Reissue edition, 2015

11) Section 4: Henry David Thoreau's quote from *A Week on the Concord and Merrimack Rivers.* New York: Charles Scribner's Sons, n.d.

12) Page 76: From "Run Through the Jungle" by John Fogerty/ Creedence Clearwater Revival from *Cosmo's Factory*, Fantasy Records, released April 1970

About the Author

I grew up in southeastern Florida where hot summer days sizzled and summer nights' humid lips of jasmine pressed against my frosted bedroom jalousies. An aspiring athlete, I wanted to play for the Milwaukee Braves—I thought Hank Aaron was poetry in motion. Well, songwriter for a garage band, later I found myself a college sophomore writing poetry and a founding member of a group of poets and artists known as the Immanentists. Though somewhat eclectic, we were a blend of European Surrealism with a Native American sensibility who believed that through language and paint we could attain spiritual fusion with the natural world. After reading The Immanentist Anthology, the great French poet, Yves Bonnefoy, said that Immanentism was the most exciting poetry he had seen from the US in decades. What a thrill! I remained in contact with Yves until his death in 2016. Eventually, I drove a yellow Ryder truck from West Palm Beach to Baltimore to attend the graduate Writing Seminars at Johns Hopkins University where I made a beeline to the National Gallery in DC to marvel at the wondrous creations by Rembrandt, Vermeer, Monet, Manet, and Odilon Redon. Baltimore became my heaven with snow. Inspired by Andrew Marvell, William Blake, Walt Whitman, Federico García Lorca, Gabriela Mistral, Pablo Neruda, Eunice Odio, Sándor Kányádi, Kristina Ehin, plus hundreds of others, I now write poems about anything and everything. Along the way I've learned that to write poetry is to love, and to love is to write poetry.

—Alan Britt

Alan has published 25 books of poetry and teaches English/ Creative Writing at Towson University.

Publications by Alan Britt

Books

Garden of Earthly Delights
Guilty Pleasures
The Tavern of Lost Souls
Emergency Room
Optical Illusions
Dream Highway
Gunpowder for Single-ball Poems
Ode to Nothing/Óda a semmihez (bilingual) Translated into Hungarian by Paul Sohar
Crossing the Walt Whitman Bridge/Traversând podul Walt Whitman (bilingual) Translated into Romanian by Flavia Cosma
Violin Smoke/Hegedűfüst (bilingual) Translated into Hungarian by Paul Sohar
Lost Among the Hours
Parabola Dreams (with Silvia Scheibli)
Alone with the Terrible Universe
Greatest Hits
Hurricane
Vegetable Love
Vermilion
Infinite Days
Amnesia Tango
Bodies of Lightning
The Afternoon of the Light
I Suppose the Darkness Is Ours
Ashes in the Flesh
I Ask for Silence Also

Anthologies (Editor)

We Are You: Poetry
Alianza: 5 U.S. Poets in Ecuador
Mantras: An Anthology of Immanentist Poetry

Poetry Journal (Editor)

Black Moon: Poetry of Imagination

Editor-in-Chief/Poetry Editor/Associate Editor

We Are You Project International
The Loch Raven Review
Ethos Literary Journal (India)

Miscellaneous

Poetry and the Concept of Maya by David Churchill
(Based upon the poetry of Alan Britt)

Books by Alan Britt available from **Magical Jeep Distributing:** www.magicaljeep.com/s/shop and www.magicaljeep.com/shop/britt/10

www.ingramcontent.com/pod-product-compliance
Lightning Source LLC
LaVergne TN
LVHW050935080826
845145LV00004B/1266